Fishing On
The Other Side

A Guide To Being The
Church In
The Digital Age

Mark Weible

WHAT OTHERS ARE SAYING

This book is not only timely but also coming from a practitioner. I have known Mark for a number of years as a learner, practical leader, and intentional collaborator. The insights he presents in this book are coming from what he practices daily and will help ministry leaders remain relevant in a changing environment. I appreciate Mark for writing.

Bekele Shanko
Cru VP, Global Church Movements
Chairman, GACX

For the past 20 years in church planting, Mark has been a close friend and one of the most valuable assets in ministry for me. Through his expertise and knowledge in internet marketing, I was able to reach and engage people with the gospel that I would have never been able to do on my own.   You'll find this book a tremendous read and a valuable resource for your entire church.

Hal Haller
Pastor, Living Hope Church
Stamford, CT

Mark opens the doors to the world for our churches who once thought they could only participate in missions and ministry through giving of their finances. The world of the internet and technology is not beyond their reach. Even the smallest churches can connect with the millennials and the Muslims that live across the street or the other side of the world. Thank you Mark for opening doors for our churches.

John Kuespert
Director of Missions, Pasco Baptist Association
Land O Lakes FL

As one who enjoyed fishing with Mark's father, I can vouch for his new approach in sharing the Gospel. Finding different ways to introduce the Savior will always be needed and Mark has provided a helpful guidebook for those interested in being "fishers of men".

Kenneth F. Brown, Retired Minister
San Antonio, TX

Mark Weible has a passion for helping churches present their church to the community in the best possible way through social media. Mark has the ability to communicate in layman's terms effective ways to improve church communications using Facebook, twitter, and more. He has helped the churches I work through workshops and personal consultations to develop a strategy for communicating to their sphere of influence on the web. Mark is a godly husband, father, church planter and overall SM geek. As you read this book, your church will benefit greatly from his experience and knowledge.

Mike Hoffmann, Lead Missional Strategist,
Brevard Baptist Association,
Melbourne, FL

DEDICATION:

To Walt Weible, the man who taught me more
about fishing than anyone other than Jesus.

CONTENTS

FOREWORD

It is a pleasure to recommend to you this new work by Mark Weible, the Strategic Director of the Renovate Group and the Renovate National Church Revitalization Conferences. I have known Mark for over twenty-five years and had tried to hire him five times during that time. Finally, in God's providence the Lord allowed me to join Mark in Orlando as I became the Executive Director of Missions for the Greater Orlando Baptist Association. Once together we sought ways to increase our influence towards the helping of plateaued or declining churches in the field of Church Revitalization and Renewal. As the Founder and Directional Leader of the Renovate Group and the Renovate National Church Revitalization Conferences, I needed someone who would share the same commitment to see these churches brought back to life and vitality. Mark Weible was the person God choose to be day to day director of all of the ins and out of the Renovate Resources and Conferences. I could not do all that we have been able to do if it were not for the excellence Mark brings to the cause of church revitalization.

That is why I am so excited to commend his new book *Fishing on The Other Side: A Guide to Being the Church in the Digital Age*. Mark declares, we live in a world where people are crying out for help, and we, the Church, have the help that they need, but lately we have not been very successful at sharing the gospel with those who really want it. This book will show you how to take the journey towards revitalization through learning how to utilize the emerging technologies available to the local church and embracing the digital age. We often have referred to Mark as the Search Engine Optimization Jedi Master. Mark effortlessly wields his light saber around the digital world helping churches in need find the revitalization tools and methodologies through RenovateConference.org. While so many show appreciations to me as the leader of the Renovate Group, nothing would ever have happened if it were not for the skills that this fine servant of the Lord brings to the cause. Do not miss out on the key chapter dealing with your church's website. Far too many churches squandered their chance to embrace a larger audience simply because they have an outdated website that is not responsive to the intended audience searching for a church. This one chapter is worth the price of the book. You may not have thought about this before, but your church's website is your modern-day fellowship hall. Most of your initial contacts with prospects will come from people first checking you out via the web long before they check you out in person.

This book will help you build an outreach strategy that is designed for today's digital inquirer that wants to know Jesus long before they are interested in knowing you and your church. Learning how to utilize digital marketing as well as social networking will bring your church into the new century and technological age. These tools will allow you a greater impact in one's community for the cause of Jesus. If I was beginning a new journey as a pastor called to revitalize the church this is one of the first books I would read. In fact, I would keep it right next to my Bible. I would have the Word of God as a tool to reach the lost and *Fishing on The Other Side* to learn new ways to connect with them where they are and not where we hope them to be which is knocking down our doors because you just arrived.

Read this book initially as a quick read to get you up to speed regarding the world of digital media. Secondly, then walk through the text acquiring the new skills that will help your church survive in the digital age. Pastors just cannot hide their heads in the sand any longer displaying an ignorance towards useful technologies which can help their church. This book will help you and your staff learn how to reach unreached prospects that before were invisible to your church. In order to follow Jesus in the digital age, we will need to detach ourselves from some of our outdated outreach methods and tools that worked well in the past but are not as well suited for the present. We will do this because we love Jesus and we love the people that He died to save. We have been fishing on one side of the boat for so long that we've developed a preference for doing things in a certain way even if that way is no longer working. Let's face it, the world has changed and is still undergoing rapid change, but churches typically are slow to embrace change. Imagine that you are one of Jesus' disciples sitting in a boat. You have been fishing all night with no results and along comes the resurrected Christ telling you that if you would just cast your nets on the other side of the boat that you will catch some fish. What would your response be? Would you be willing to try something new or would you keep doing what you've been doing even though you are coming up empty every time? We must keep fishing for those who do not know Jesus, those who need Jesus and those who Jesus says come follow me.

Tom Cheyney, Founder & Directional Leader

The Renovate Group

The Renovate National Church Revitalization Conferences

ACKNOWLEDGMENTS

Thank you, my dear wife Tammy, for encouraging me to write this book. I would have never completed it without you. Thank you, Tom Cheyney, for inspiring me and instilling confidence that I could do this. I also want to thank my employer – Greater Orlando Baptist Association for providing the experience where I gained and tested most of the knowledge in these pages and for allowing me to take a sabbatical to finish writing. Thanks to Jannell Pace for editing and correcting my many mistakes. Thanks to Gerald Brown for designing the cover. Most of all, I want to thank the many pastors that I've had the privilege to serve over the years. They are the ones who've listened to and implemented my crazy ideas well before they were proven. These committed servants of Jesus are the hidden source material for much of what is included in this book

INTRODUCTION
FIRST, SOME FISHING LESSONS

"Come, follow me," Jesus said, "and I will send
you out to fish for people.
(Matthew 4:19, NIV)

My father loved to go fishing and we went
fishing as often as we could when I was a boy.
We used to practice casting with a spinning reel
in our back yard, but we never caught any fish
there. There was no water and there were no
fish in the back yard. In order to catch fish, we
had to go where the fish were. This is our first
fishing lesson: Jesus did not wait for people to
come to Him so we must go to them.

*Jesus went through all the towns and villages,
teaching in their synagogues, proclaiming the
good news of the kingdom and healing every
disease and sickness.* (Matthew 9:35)

He took His disciples to the people in order
to establish a pattern for the early church (and
our churches today) to follow. We can't just wait
for people to come to us. We have to go where
the people are and, more importantly, we have
to be willing to go where they want to be
reached. Jesus said, "The harvest is plentiful,
but the workers are few."[i] There are thousands

of people in close proximity to you and your church who want to be reached. They are hurting, lost, hopeless, fearful and they need the gospel. Like a grain field full of ripe wheat, they are ready to be harvested, but we have to meet them where they are.

The first disciples that Jesus called were fishermen. His invitation for them to follow Him was personalized and meaningful to them. The first part of the invitation was "come." At that point, they did not know where they were to be going, but one thing was for sure, they had to leave in order to get there. They left behind all that was familiar: their families, their homes, their friendships, their jobs and the tools of their trade– their nets. They did not know what they would be doing, but they knew that fishing for people did not involve nets. So, they left their nets and they followed Jesus. We too have to be willing to leave behind the familiar to go on a life-long adventure with Jesus. In order to follow Jesus in the digital age, we will need to detach ourselves from some of our outreach methods and tools that worked well in the past but are not as well-suited for the present. We will do this because we love Jesus and we love the people that He died to save.

Jesus loves unreached people more than we do. He hears their cries for help; He feels their pain and He has entrusted us with what they need– the gospel. Paul said, "But we have this treasure in jars of clay to show that this all-surpassing power is from God and not from us."[ii] The treasure is the gospel and we are like fragile jars of clay, carrying around inside of us, the life changing power of the gospel. The gospel is not ours to keep hidden inside of us and we are commanded by Jesus to put this treasure on display for all of the world to see:

> *"You are the light of the world. A town built on a hill cannot be hidden. Neither do people light a lamp and put it under a bowl. Instead they put it on its stand, and it gives light to everyone in the house. In the same way, let your light shine before others, that they may see your good deeds and glorify your Father in heaven.* (Matthew 5: 14-15)

We live in a world where people are crying out for help, and we, the Church, have the help that they need. Lately, however, we have not been very successful at sharing the gospel with those who really want it. Tom Cheyney writes in his book *Life After Death* that 90% of the churches in America that are in a state of decline have stopped reaching new people.[iii]

We've been fishing on one side of the boat for so long that we've developed a preference for doing things a certain way even if that way is no longer working. Let's face it, the world has changed and is still undergoing rapid change, but churches typically are slow to embrace change. Imagine that you are one of Jesus' disciples sitting in a boat. You've been fishing all night with no results and along comes the resurrected Christ telling you that if you would just cast your nets on the other side of the boat that you will catch some fish. What would your response be? Would you be willing to try something new or would you keep doing what you've been doing even though you are coming up empty every time?

Matthew was not a fisherman. When Jesus called Matthew, who was a tax collector, He did not use fishing language because that terminology would have been foreign to Matthew. Instead, Jesus went to his house and had a party with Matthew and his tax collector friends. By doing so, Jesus showed that He was a different kind of Rabbi. Rabbis were not supposed to eat a meal with or to even enter the home of people like Matthew. However, Jesus was the kind of leader who was willing to be chastised for partying with "tax collectors and sinners" while affirming their humanity and worth. At any rate, Jesus personalized the call to each individual disciple. This is our second fishing lesson: Jesus personalized the gospel to each person that he encountered. Not only do we need to go where the people are, we must

4

speak to them in ways that they will understand the gospel. Jesus gave the same message to different people in different ways.

What we say, how we say it, and even the medium we use to communicate the gospel needs to be customized to the person we are reaching. Today, it seems as if each person has their own preference for how they want to be reached. I have some friends who don't text, but they do respond to email. I have some friends who never answer their phone but are quick to respond on Facebook messenger. Some people really like it if I send them a card via old-fashioned snail mail. In order to be a good friend, it is now my responsibility to discover and use each friends' preferred communication platform. If I really care about them, I will communicate with them using whatever method that they prefer instead of expecting them to use mine. Since I don't have a standard approach to communicating with my friends, I don't have a standard approach to sharing the gospel either.

My Dad had a friend who was a professional fishing guide. He always seemed to know where the fish were, what they would be biting and the best ways to catch them. Elroy was the only one that I knew who could out-fish my Dad. When Dad asked his buddy the secret to becoming a better fisherman, Elroy answered,

"Walt, you just have to learn to think like a fish." This is our third fishing lesson: We need to try to see the world from the perspective of someone who does not yet know Christ in order to communicate the gospel with them on their level wherever they are. That does not mean that we adopt another person's world view in order to reach them. It means that we just try to understand them and to understand where they are coming from. My Dad's friend Elroy learned to think like a fish, but he never sprouted gills and jumped into the water. Just the same, if we insist that everyone meet us where we are, talk the way that we want to talk and do what we want to do, then we've become self-centered and we are not following the example that was set by Jesus.

In case you are wondering, this is not a book about fishing. And just to clear things up, we are not talking about phishing or trolling either. Fishing on the Other Side is about following Jesus and obeying His command to make disciples. Jesus told His first disciples that if they were to follow Him, He would teach them how to fish for people. They already knew how to catch fish, but now they would be catching people with the gospel. The principles for reaching people and catching fish are similar. What I've learned about fishing, I've also learned to apply to making disciples of Jesus:

1. You have to go where the people are.
2. You have to use different techniques and tools to reach different kinds of people.
3. To reach a lost person, it helps to think like a lost person.

This book has a particular focus on utilizing the technological tools available to churches today to reach people whose lives are shaped by those same tools. Included in these pages are stories for illustrative purposes some of them really happened and some are like parables that serve to drive home a point. This is not a book about technology, but it is about the intersection of people and technology in the digital age. Some of the digital resources referred to can be found in the appendix. In a time when the majority of churches are in a state of decline all over America and the old tools and techniques of evangelism do not seem to be working as well, it is time that we adjust our techniques and start fishing on the other side.

CHAPTER ONE
SOCIAL EVANGELISM

He called out to them, "Friends, haven't you any
fish?"
"No," they answered.
He said, "Throw your net on the right side of the boat
and you will find some." When they did, they were
unable to haul the net in because of the large number of
fish.
(John 21: 5-6, NIV)

Evangelism literally means "to tell good news."
A Christian witness is one who tells the Good
News of what Jesus Christ has done for them
personally. When something good happens to
you, you naturally want to share it with those
you know and love. It is not complicated at all,
but churches often use complicated methods to
train their members to share the gospel. I am not
against evangelism training, but most of the
evangelism training that I have been exposed to
over-complicates evangelism to the point that
the training itself has the opposite effect of its
purpose. When you use over-complicated
methods to train people in evangelism, you
teach them that evangelism is too difficult for
the average Believer.

Chuck Kelley, President of New Orleans
Baptist Theological Seminary, at a gathering of

church leaders in Orlando, Florida asked this question, "How many of you grandparents out there had to be trained to tell your friends about your grandkids?[iv]" As you can imagine, not a single person raised their hand. If the Gospel really is good news to you, then you will surely want to share the best thing that ever happened to you with the people that you know. We freely share much less important things with even our most casual acquaintances: "Hey everyone, today is free donut day at Krispy Kreme!" We may shout that message out to our co-workers down on the cube farm, text it to our friends or even post it on social media for the whole world to see. Free donuts at Krispy Kreme is really good news and we are likely to share messages like that in the most natural method of communication available to us. Evangelism is a social activity and people will share the good news of Jesus the same way they share any other news.

Using the internet to evangelize is no different than any other form of evangelism. It is simply going where the people are and sharing the best thing that ever happened to you. The internet does not take the place of face to face communication, it merely enhances it. It is a form of communication and a tool for social interaction. People like getting positive life-changing information online.

In early Twentieth Century America, people socialized on the front porches of their homes. They did not have televisions, computers, or air conditioners. The front porch was a place to hang out, drink some lemonade, listen to the radio and chat with neighbors. When small groups of people from local churches came walking down the sidewalk, they had an open invitation to engage their neighbors in conversation. Going door to door was the most effective means of evangelism at that time. It was socially acceptable to talk with your neighbor over the picket fence. The very fact that the neighbors were sitting on the porch was an open invitation to engage them in a conversation about any subject, whether it be the weather or the gospel.

In the early Twenty-First Century, the internet, social media and phones have become the new front porch for many people. For most Americans, it has become socially acceptable to engage people in conversation through texting and social media just as it was once considered to be socially acceptable to engage people in conversation on their front porch.

To be missional is to think and act like a missionary. Effective missionaries are students of language and culture. Missionaries want to know how to communicate with people in their target communities. They need to know what forms of communication are considered to be culturally acceptable. They want to know how to engage people in spiritual conversations. Missionaries want to discover the most effective means of sharing the gospel with people representing the people group or population segment that they are trying to reach. One of the tasks of a missionary is to discover the preferred method and place of communication with his or her target group. In the early Twentieth Century, the front porch was a good place to begin a conversation, but it didn't always end there. Sometimes, a visitor would get invited inside the house for a piece of pie, or they may have continued the conversation at another time in another place over some other activity.

In the Twenty-First Century, a lot of conversations begin online. The internet has become the new front porch. Many of us have social media "friends" that we've never actually met face to face. They may be friends of friends, distant relatives, long distance co-workers or simply people interested in the same things that we are interested in. Unless you do it in a creepy way, it is often considered okay to like or comment on a person's post online. Most people are not going to think it rude of you or intrusive for you to respond to someone's question or to offer suggestions for a need that they have posted. For most of us, online conversations are just as natural as front porch conversations were a couple of generations ago. In many cases, online conversations merely enhance offline friendships and relationships. The internet can be a tool for helping us to get to know others better and a great way to help us to share some good news with our friends.

Evangelism is a word that I hear almost as often in the business culture as in Christian circles. A customer evangelist is one who spreads the good news about a product or service that he or she recommends without any thought of personal gain or reward.[v] Customer evangelists will spread the word about worthwhile businesses through word of mouth, on their blogs, in social media, and any other way that they communicate with their friends. Why? Because they like their friends and they want to share their experiences with their friends. No one has to train them to be evangelistic, they just love to share good news.

As you can imagine, businesses want to have lots of customer evangelists. They want to get as many people as possible out there talking about their products and services. Some businesses have people serving in high levels of their companies with the title of "Chief Evangelist." The job of the chief evangelist is to recruit and encourage customer evangelists while creating a sense of community for those who freely share the good news of their company's offerings. As you can imagine, the internet has become the preferred method of message delivery for customer evangelists as an enhancement to face-to-face word of mouth interactions. The internet is cheap, readily available, easy to use and widely accepted.

Our family recently stayed in a hotel near the Smoky Mountains on our vacation. Before we booked a room that we were going to stay in for seven days, we did a lot of research online. When we found a good price and location, we read the description of the hotel and room type on the hotel's website and we read reviews of the hotel on third party websites. One of the things that impressed us was that someone from the hotel staff responded to almost every review - good or bad. We could tell from the reviews and the responses that the staff and especially the hotel's general manager really seemed to care about their guests. We could tell that it was very important to them that each guest have a positive experience. When we stayed at the hotel, we had a problem on our first day that would have made the rest of our stay a little uncomfortable. I brought this issue to the attention of the general manager and she quickly offered a solution that far exceeded our expectations. We were so grateful for the way that the GM and staff resolved our issue that we immediately became evangelists for that particular hotel. Not only did I write a glowing review on a couple of websites, but we also told our family and friends how well we were treated when we got back home. If anyone asks me where to stay in the Smoky Mountains, I have a recommendation for them. And even if they don't ask, anyone that I know traveling to that region will hear about our experience.

Christians want to share their faith with their friends because they like their friends and they want them to experience the fullness of Christ. They don't want to go to training classes to memorize a presentation and feel pressured to "present" the gospel to strangers. Evangelism is all about sharing the good news of the gospel. The gospel is more than a message to be delivered, it is a life-changing experience to be shared. Sharing the gospel should be the most natural thing in the world for a believer in Christ. It should not feel contrived or come across as a sales pitch. Most of all, our gospel sharing should not be a one size fits all approach.

Read through the evangelistic encounters of Jesus in the Gospel of John and you will discover that each encounter started out as a unique conversation. Sometimes it was initiated by Jesus and at other times the person being evangelized started the conversation. While each evangelistic conversation was different, Jesus always led the person to understand their need for salvation. Take a look at these examples:

- John 3: 1-21 – Nicodemus
- John 4: 1-27 – Samaritan Woman
- John 5: 1-14 – Paralyzed Man
- John 9: 1-6 – Blind Man

In each of these passages, Jesus simply met the people where they were, addressed their individual situation and showed them their need for salvation. Conversations like these can happen today in person, on the phone or online. In the examples listed above, Jesus was doing front-line evangelism. He was reaching people who did not yet have a network of relationships with others who had already experienced this amazing life transformation. Once these new believers accepted the Gospel of Jesus, they shared the good news of salvation with their families, friends, and acquaintances. Evangelism moved from the front-line along relational lines.

Paul was also a front-line evangelist. In Philippi, a jailer started a spiritual conversation by asking Paul and Silas, "Sirs, what must I do to be saved?"[vi] Not only did that man became a follower of Jesus that night, but so did his entire household.[vii] Previously, Paul had helped a woman named Lydia come to know Christ. As a result, her entire household became followers of Jesus too.[viii] When the people that we share the gospel with share it with others who then share with others, evangelism goes viral!

Several years ago, while speaking at a Christian college, I shared with the students a process that I called "reverse engineered evangelism." I developed this system after realizing that most evangelism training begins with the assumption that the person sharing the gospel and the person hearing the gospel are complete strangers and have not had any previous interaction. For most Believers, the prospect of sharing something as profound and deeply personal as the gospel with a complete stranger is terrifying. I developed this process after hearing my former boss ask the question, "How are we teaching people how to evangelize the people that they love?" This caused me to think and ask myself, "Why don't we love everyone that we are evangelizing? Wouldn't that make evangelism much easier." So, here is what I shared with the students:

- Evangelize those that you love.
- Love those that you serve.
- Serve those that you know.
- Get to know those that you don't (love, serve or know).

The students responded with enthusiasm and relief. This process incorporates establishing and building relationships, meeting people's needs, demonstrating the love of Christ and verbally sharing the message of the gospel. On that day, those students conveyed to me that following this pattern of evangelism seemed more natural, less contrived and less stressful. It seemed to be more authentic and less awkward than trying to talk to complete strangers about spiritual life change.

With the tools that we have available to us today, we have the opportunity to reach people all over the world through viral evangelism. When a message goes viral, it spreads contagiously and multiplies exponentially. While business marketers would love to create viral messages and to see their brands become household terms, most viral messages are organic. Organic messages are created by individuals who are not being paid to create such messages. When an organic message goes viral it is because the message is perceived to be of some value to the recipient and assumed that the sender has no ulterior motives other than passing along some helpful information or entertaining content.

When followers of Jesus utilize the Twenty-First Century tools available to us while following Biblical principles, we can see the gospel go viral resulting in more people being discipled, more churches being planted and more churches getting revitalized. Churches can become more effective and individuals more fruitful in fulfilling their missional mandate. Many are already doing this well, but others are still scratching their heads and wondering why they are not catching any "fish". Then, Jesus comes and says, "Throw your net on the right side of the boat and you will find some."[ix].

CHAPTER TWO
OUR CHURCH WEBSITE

At the dawn of the Twenty-First Century, I was enjoying some appetizers with a couple of friends at a restaurant near the Orlando airport. We were talking about the challenges and opportunities that church leaders were facing in this new era. We got into talking about something called "web 2.0," which is a term that pre-dated social media. We were exploring this interesting concept that the internet was maturing and moving beyond businesses and organizations simply posting their brochure content to static web pages and expecting people to read them. Web 2.0 was a concept based on the idea that individuals would want to interact with internet content and not just read it. We started seeing it in the proliferation of blogging platforms where anyone could become a journalist, and anyone could comment on the content that was posted. As we discussed the underlying reasons for this, one of my friends made a profound observation. "You know," he said, "Twenty-First Century humans will exist in cyberspace as well as time and space and the Church will need to meet them in both places." Almost twenty years later, I am finding that many churches are still struggling with reaching people in these two worlds.

The earliest church websites were usually nothing more than an online brochure. Churches viewed their website as just another place to put the same information that they already had in print somewhere else. Little thought was given to who would be reading the information, what they would be looking for and why. Back then, having a website was just another way of showing that your church was cool, hip or at least staying up to date with technology. The way most people found your church website was by looking for the church's URL in very tiny print at the bottom of the Sunday bulletin.

Now, most church leaders are more sophisticated than that. They know that nearly all of the people who visit a church gathering for the first time will visit the church's website first[x]. They know that they can use web analytics to find out how many people are visiting the church's website, where they are coming from, what they are searching for, how long they stay on the website and how many pages they view. They also know that fewer than one percent of the people who visit the church's website will ever visit one of the church's worship services. Website conversion expert, Neil Patel, has stated that 99% of the people who visit a typical website do not convert. In Patel's terminology, a conversion happens when a website visitor buys something or takes a desired action.[xi] If the purpose of a church website is to get the people who visit the website to come to church, then the average church website fails 99% of the time. But we can change that!

Why does your church website exist and what is its purpose? Was your church's website created for your current church members or was it designed primarily to reach new people? A properly developed website will serve several groups of people including current church members, people searching for a church and people looking for something offered by your church. How do you evaluate the effectiveness of your church website? One way to do so would be to ask the question, "If our website were an employee, what would be included in its job description." If you were to give your church website an annual review, what criteria would you use to determine if it was doing its job effectively. If your website were a person, how would you know whether to give him or her a raise or to fire them?

Try this simple test: look at the home page of your current church website and count how many times a first-person pronoun (we or us) is used. Then, count how many times the second-person pronoun (you) occurs on the page. You can easily count word occurrences on a web page from most internet browsers by using the command+f or ctrl+f keys and typing a word in the search box. Try this on several pages of your website and compare the number of occurrences of first- to second-person pronouns. If the website is more about "we" and less about "you" then it is more church-focused than visitor-focused.

Here is another test: Look to see if your church location, especially city and state, is one of the first things that you see on your church's website. Current church members already know where the church meets, but potential visitors need to know immediately if they've even landed on the right website. For example, if you conduct an internet search for "Calvary Church," you will notice on the search engine result pages that there are many churches with "Calvary" in their name. Some of these results will have the location clearly marked with city and state either in the head title link that takes you to their site or in the search snippet below the link. For some of the search results, it is difficult to tell whether or not that particular "Calvary" is even in your neighborhood, city or state. If you were a potential visitor, which one would you click? Try clicking on several of the links in the search results. When you land on a church web page, look at it through the eyes of someone unfamiliar with the church. Does the church website clearly indicate the church's location without having to scroll to the bottom of the page or click to another page?

Now, go back to your own church website. How does it look to a prospective visitor? Is the location clearly indicated at the top of the page? Ideally, the location should be in the header, next to or below the logo. Is there a phone number? Are there links to social media pages? Is there easy to find information about what to expect or what to do on Sunday mornings including worship times? These are all things that you can look for as you diagnose your church website for visitor friendliness.

An effective church website will provide helpful information to at least three groups of people: current church members and regular attenders, potential visitors and the general public. Think about the different groups of people who may visit your church's website and look at the site from each group's perspective. Members and regular attenders like to see up to date information about church activities. They may want to listen to or watch a recent sermon. Current attenders would like information on when and where small groups are meeting. A calendar of events is helpful to all of your web visitors. If you do not provide up to date information for the people who are already attending your church, they may be the least likely people to visit your church website.

You may be thinking, "How often should we update our church website." The answer to that question can be determined by another question: How often do you want people to visit your church website? If you want people to visit every day, then the website content should be updated every day. What would you do if you subscribed to a local newspaper and the content of that paper never changed from day to day? It would not be worth your time and effort to even open the newspaper if you knew that the contents of today's paper would be the same as yesterday. That is the way that people think about your website. Why bother visiting again if nothing ever changes?

Other than your current members and attenders, there are people looking at your church website who are thinking about visiting your church for the first time. Prospective church visitors want to know the time and location of up-coming worship services and what to expect in regard to worship style. They may want to know if there are separate activities for children and if dress is casual or more formal. The church website should provide all of this information and more in an obvious, easy to find location. A tab or navigation button simply titled "What to Expect on Your First Visit" or something similar should lead to a single webpage with all of the pertinent information for first-time visitors. A potential visitor should not have to click through several pages to get worship times, directions, expectations, child check-in procedures, etc. The best practice is to put all of this information on a printer-friendly page that makes it easy for the prospect to carry with them on their first visit.

A third group of people visiting your church website includes members of the general public, who are searching the internet for something that they need, but did not necessarily think of looking for it at a church. For example, if your church runs a preschool and someone does a search for a preschool in their area, your church website may just offer the most relevant content to what they are looking for. This particular person is not looking for a church to attend on Sunday mornings, they just need someone to take care of their child while they are at work and your church offers that service. What does your church website say to this group of people? Does it dispel or reinforce untrue stereotypes about Christians? Does it make a good statement about, not only the preschool, but the church itself? What needs to be changed in order to make a better first impression?

The general public has broader interests than just attending your church. There are people out there searching the internet for information, activities and services that your church provides. Let's say that someone has been listening to a national talk show host talking about how to achieve financial freedom. They find out that this person offers classes all over the country and your church offers these classes or seminars. When an internet search is done - boom! There's your church's website at the top of the search results page because someone posted content relevant to what this person was searching for. Once again, they were not looking for a church to attend, but they don't mind taking a financial freedom class at a church if it is near their home. By serving the community in this manner, your church's website is accomplishing one of its goals – to help the church to connect with people who do not yet know that they need a church. Now, I would never advocate a "bait and switch" approach, but I do believe that the gospel is best shared in the context of relationships and what better way to begin a relationship with someone than meeting a big need in their life.

Your church website will likely provide one of the first impressions of your church to people who are looking for a church family and others in the community. Jesus taught His disciples to serve one another. In John 13, He demonstrated this by washing their feet and commanding them to do the same. The church website can be an incredible tool for serving others and increasing the effectiveness of the ministry of the church. Those who work on the website should consider themselves as webservants instead of webmasters. Through your church website, you can provide valuable services to all of your target audiences.

One example of great service is offering online giving. Fewer people carry checkbooks and cash nowadays and people who want to give are inconvenienced if your church does not offer online giving. Not only do your regulars want to give online, but there are others who may not live in proximity to the church who want to support the church's work. If your church's community is ever affected by a natural or man-made disaster, people from all over the world will want to give to your relief efforts and by offering online giving you are serving them while you are also serving your community. There really is no good reason for a church not to offer online giving.

Not offering online giving can cause your church to miss out on someone's generosity. A friend of mine wanted to make a large gift to his church on December 31. He had just received a royalty check and wanted give to his church, and have it deducted from that year's taxes. His church did not offer electronic giving through the church website. When he visited another church's website that allowed for online giving, he was obliged to give through that church instead. The following Sunday he explained to his pastor why he gave a large gift to another church. My friend's church soon started offering online giving!

Online registration for children's ministry and special events is another example of providing excellent service to your members and visitors. Many churches now require parents to fill out registration and medical forms before leaving the babies in the nursery or entering children's worship. My wife and I have attended many churches where the child check-in process for first time visitors was chaotic at best. Since most first-time visitors will visit the church website before they attend a worship service or event, why not offer online registration for children's ministry? Building an online form is not at all difficult with most content management website platforms. The Renovate Group actually offers low-cost websites to churches with easy to use online forms at www.OurChurch.Website.

Another way of serving your target audiences is to utilize the blogging feature that is built into most CMS based websites. CMS stands for Content Management System and is often used as the backend platform for website management. Blogs can be used to keep various groups in the church informed of important details relating to church administration, training, outreach opportunities, etc. Pastors can use blogs to expand the impact of weekly sermons by encouraging the church to live out what they learn. Most pastors that I know have a hard time reducing their sermon content to the allotted time for their weekly worship services. A blog allows pastors to expand on their weekly sermons while encouraging practical application in daily life. Using an RSS Feed, blog content can be syndicated across the web and users can subscribe to blog content via email and text notification. There is an excellent free tool for content syndication provided by google at www.FeedBurner.com. Blogs can also be used as podcast engines simply by enclosing an audio or video file attachment.

A church website and other web-based tools can be used for internal private communication as well. Let's face it, people today are very busy, and they don't have time to attend lots of church meetings. One way to serve the body of Christ is to reduce or eliminate team or committee meetings by utilizing private pages on your church website. The budget team leader can upload the latest spreadsheet and invite team members to make their suggestions utilizing a private web page that requires user login. Groups can use live chat on their phones so that meetings can be held anywhere. Online meeting tools can be used to have virtual meetings that save time for more important things like family.

Many churches are now using online video training for volunteers and staff. Videos can be produced in-house with inexpensive equipment and uploaded to video sharing websites such as YouTube and Vimeo. These videos can then be imbedded into the church website by copying and pasting some simple html code. They can be made public or kept private. Churches can also subscribe to video training services offered by several church support organizations such as www.Renovate.Digital.

An effective church website will meet the needs of current members and regular attenders, prospective new comers as well as members of the general public who happen to find the church website while looking for something non-church related. The people who work on the website will need to take the posture of a foot-washing servant and go out of their way to make the website useful and inviting. If your church is doing all of this, great! Now, how do you get people to visit your church website to begin with? Stick around because chapter 3 is all about Search Engine Optimization.

CHAPTER THREE
SEARCH ENGINE OPTIMIZATION

Barry had not been to church since he was a child. He spent most of his life thinking that he did not need God, and even doubting God's existence. All of that changed when his wife threatened to leave him if he did not get his life together. Barry loved his wife and did not want to lose her. But he felt his life had no direction and that his family deserved something better. He felt empty and alone. Barry began to cry out to God for help. He decided to take his family to church one Sunday. He hoped that the church would have something to offer them and maybe could help keep his family together. He had a friend who really seemed to enjoy being a part of a church in their area, but he couldn't remember the name of the church or where exactly it was located.

Using his phone, Barry did a Google search for "churches near me." One of the top results was a church with a name that sounded like the one that his friend was attending. He clicked the link and saw that the church had a website that looked good on his phone. Everything was pretty straight-forward and easy to understand. He was able to easily find the location and worship gathering start time. So, he loaded up his family and took them with him to visit his friend's church. Volunteers in the parking lot helped them find a parking spot and they pointed out the signs directing them to the building entrance. Outside, there was a welcome tent where a they met a friendly hostess, who took them inside, helped them check-in their kids and escorted Barry and his wife into the worship center. Barry spotted his friend and his wife, and they sat down next to them. Overall, this church visit was a good experience for Barry and his family. They enjoyed the music, even though they weren't familiar with the songs, the people seemed to be friendly and the pastor seemed to speak directly to the needs in their life. Barry and his family decided to come back. Barry, his wife and kids all came to know Christ through the ministry of that church. Barry's story is not unique, and it illustrates how a friend and a church did a lot of things right.

Barry's smooth first visit to his friend's church did not happen by accident. There was a lot of work that went on behind the scenes to make sure that Barry and his family would have a good experience that Sunday. If the church had not invested time and money putting together a quality mobile-friendly website, Barry's family may not have attended church services that morning. Not only that, but if someone had not taken the time to make sure that the website was search engine friendly, Barry may not have even found his friend's church to begin with. The discipline of making a website search friendly is called Search Engine Optimization or SEO. There exists an entire industry of SEO experts who work extensively to make sure that certain websites rank for certain keywords or search queries and many churches seem to be oblivious of its existence. To use Jesus' fishing metaphor, it's time to cast our nets on the SEO side of the boat.

The term, "search engine optimization" is

somewhat of a misnomer. Unless you are a search engineer, you can't actually control what search engines do. However, you can optimize your church website to make it easier for search engines to crawl, index and display information about your church. You'll want to do this because, since 2000, search engines have been the #1 source of information gathering in America. Internet search engines are relied upon more than family or friends as sources of information.[xii] It is simply good stewardship of church resources and good missional strategy for churches to make sure that their information is discoverable over the internet through SEO.

Sometimes SEO gets a bad rap and churches shy away from doing SEO because of the reputation of some search engine optimizers as being spammers. Actually, there are two basic types of SEO: white hat and black hat techniques. As the titles imply the white hats are the good guys while the black hats are the bad guys. The white hats follow the rules, meeting search engine guidelines and are truly interested in making internet search more useful to the end users. Black hats practice search engine manipulation by exploiting holes in the search engine algorithms and misrepresenting the websites that they are trying to promote. Churches should never be involved in any black hat SEO strategies nor should they have anything to do with people who practice this evil art.

A search engine is simply a computer program that is designed to search the internet for information. That information is organized into an index, much like what you would find in the back of a book. However, instead of displaying information in an alphabetical table, the search engine sorts information according to relevance to search queries and displays it on web pages called search engine results pages (SERP's). A simple search query may produce thousands of pages containing hundreds of thousands of results. Search engines are so good at returning relevant results, that most people do not look beyond the first page and may hardly ever look below the fold (top half) of the first page of search results. Therefore, if a particular web page does not appear near the top of the first search engine results page, its content is not likely to be seen by anyone using a search engine. Furthermore, since more people are used to getting more of their information through internet searches, if they can't find your church on a search engine, the assumption is that either the church is poorly run, or it does not exist.

Search engines rank results based on what the search engine's algorithms determine to be the most relevant to the search query. Try this: do an internet search for your church's name and see where your church website ranks in the search results. Are you #1? Great! If not, try adding the name of the city that your church is located in (example: "Grace Church Orlando"). If your church website ranks in the top three organic (non-paid) results, that's good! But not everyone knows the name of your church.

Try doing a search for "church near me" without the quotes. What results did you get? Was your church listed? The results for this type of query will differ based on your location and the type of device (phone, tablet, laptop, etc.) and internet connection that you are using. If you are not physically located near the church address when you conduct this search, your church website may not rank at all. If you are in the church parking lot and searching for "church near me" on your phone, your church's listing should show in one of the top map or organic results. If not, you have an optimization problem that is easy to fix.

As search engines crawl the web looking for information to index, they often discover, index and display information regarding the location of businesses and organizations. This information may be gleaned from the organization's website or cited in local business directories such as yellow pages. Google, Bing and Yahoo allow local businesses and organizations to input their location and information directly via their free business listing services.

The local business listings included on search engine results pages are near the top, usually below or next to a map showing the results in the local area (see image next page). Usually there are only three local business results displayed on the SERP's. This grouping is called the three-pack. The search engines algorithmically pick three results to go in the three-pack based on information provided to the search engines, relevancy to the search query, physical proximity of the searcher to the address on the listing, the number and quality of reviews, as well as the quality of the organization's website. I like to call the three-pack the low hanging fruit for search engine optimization, because it is easy for churches to impact their ranking through each search engine's local business listing. See the appendix of this book for more information on how to access these free services.

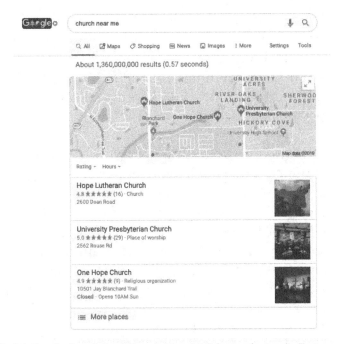

Fig 3.1 Google Search for "Church Near Me" from a laptop in East Orange County, FL. Google and the Google logo are registered trademarks of Google LLC, used with permission.

What are some other ways that people search the internet for local churches? Try searching for "church in… [your zip code]" or "church on… [your church's street]. How about "church near… [well known landmark]" These are all common internet searches for churches conducted by people who are looking for a church to visit. How does your church rank for these queries? If your church is not ranking well, some simple SEO can probably fix the problem. Bear in mind that most people who are looking for a church want to find one in close proximity to where they live. Usually that is less than a fifteen-minute drive. That is why it is important to optimize your church's website for geographic and landmark terms relevant to the person conducting the search.

How does your church perform in searches conducted by people who are not searching for a church, but searching for something your church has to offer? These could be potential evangelistic contacts who could be reached through one of your church's ministries. A church with an archery club, for example, could reach new people simply by providing information on the church website about archery. A recent Google search for "archery club" resulted in a local church being listed near the top (above the fold) of the first search engine results page in that area.

Hopefully, by now, you've conducted several internet searches for keywords and phrases that are important to your target audiences. These kinds of searches can be helpful in giving you a general idea of how your website is performing in internet search. However, you can get a false sense of security by conducting several internet searches on the same device that you actively access your church's website. Over the past several years, search engines have been delivering more personalized search results. The web pages that you see on search engine results pages are likely to be influenced by such things as: your web browsing history; your previous internet searches; your physical location; your participation in social media; your friends' social media recommendations; and more. This means that you can conduct the same search on different devices from different locations and get different results. This can make it difficult in determining where your church website actually ranks for certain keywords.

There are some good tools on the web that can help you to get an unbiased view of your church website's search engine performance. One such resource is Google Webmaster Tools[xiii]. Creating a Webmaster Tools account is free and easy to do. Once your website has been verified, you will have access to all sorts of helpful data including search query data. With a Google Webmaster Tools account, you can see search queries that cause your church website to show up in Google search results, how your website ranks for each query, and how often your website gets clicked for each search term. Similar information is also available from Bing. I also recommend conducting your test searches for your church website in an incognito browser that does not track your previous searches.

Once you get an idea of how your church

website is performing in the major search engines, you will likely see areas that are in need of improvement. A good place to start is to look at the search queries that you would like to result in top rankings for your church and think of other potential keywords that could be optimized for your church. A church should rank high for search queries that include the church name, especially if a local identifier is included in the query (ex. Calvary Church Orlando). If your church has a very common name, it may be difficult to rank in the #1 spot.

To be effective at SEO, you need to learn to think like the people in your target groups. Get into their head by asking yourself questions like, "How would I do an internet search for a church in our neighborhood?" Develop a list of potential keywords and check the search frequency of those keywords with tools like the Google Adwords Keyword Planner. Next, check the content of the pages of your church website to see if these important keywords are included in your website content in a natural manner.

There is no silver bullet in search engine optimization, however, most SEO's agree that the most important ranking factor for SEO purposes is fresh, well-written, unique and relevant content that people want to read, link to and share on social media. If your church website content is only about when and where your church meets, what you do on Sundays, etc. (as important as that is), that information will not meet the above criteria for quality, sharable content. A good church will answer the so what questions:

- You have a great church and a great website. So what good is that for me?
- You believe in the existence of God. So, what do you want me to do about that?
- You say that you have the answers to life's problems. So, what are you going to do to help me?
- You say that Jesus died on the cross to save me. So, what am I supposed to do about that?

The truth of the gospel is astounding. The message of God's grace is amazing. The Bible says that God gives His followers His authority[xiv] and power[xv] to proclaim His message to all people everywhere. Therefore, church websites should contain the most interesting, most compelling content anywhere. Search engines like to reward websites that have well written content, that has lots of links from other websites and that is being highly regarded and well discussed on various platforms online. To a search engine algorithm, such content is worthy to be ranked at the top of search engine results pages when it is deemed to be relevant to what the searcher is searching for. That is the secret sauce of SEO. Search engines index content. That is what they do.

The way that textual content is written can also have an impact on search results. Search engines are designed to discover and deliver internet content that is relevant to queries that are entered by search engine users. Search engines use algorithms to try to determine website quality, trust, relevance and overall user experience. Search engines evaluate text content much in the same way that an English teacher evaluates the quality of an essay submitted by a student. Website content that is well written with good grammar and punctuation is likely to help a page to rank higher in search results than poorly written content. If you were to submit the written content on your church website to a freshman English professor for a grade would you get an A?

Another ranking factor is trust. A web page can be deemed trustworthy if it has several inbound links from other trusted websites and is widely recommended or shared on social media. In the early days of Google, spammy webmasters would do anything to get inbound links from other websites including paying money to other website owners for those links. That kind of activity is considered to be manipulative by search engines and it violates their quality guidelines. In later years, search engines like Google started penalizing websites that participated in this kind of behavior by dropping the websites' ranking in the search results or removing such websites from their index altogether. Churches should not be involved in any spammy activities at all. Use this rule of thumb when conducting search engine optimization... If it seems wrong, it is.

Other issues affecting trust are the age and past history of the website's domain name. An older domain that has a clean record of not being spammy may rank higher than a newer domain. This is not always the case as there are hundreds of other ranking factors that search engines use to determine website quality and content relevance. Trust can also be determined by the number of quality inbound links and other factors such as brand reputation.

Other ranking factors relate to the design and functionality of a website. Search engine companies want to continually improve on the user experience. Therefore, poorly designed websites that load slowly, are difficult to navigate or don't look good on mobile devices are likely to be penalized with lower rankings in search engine results. Websites that are more secure by using Secure Socket Layer (SSL) encryption may rank higher than websites that are less secure.

To improve the search engine ranking of your church website, focus on quality content using words and phrases that people in your target audience are likely to search for, let everyone know about your website and encourage them to discuss it on social media. Make sure that the title of each page of your church website is unique, relevant to the content of the page, and contains important keywords that people are searching for. Write a descriptive snippet for each page in the "description" box of the CMS platform for each page. Google usually (but not always) uses the page title and description that you provide on their SERP's. In the following example, you can see how the website page title and description shows on Google as well as the page titles of some of the other pages on this church's website.

Church Near Sea World | Central Parkway - Orlando, FL
www.cpbcorlando.com/ ▾
We are located 5281 Central Florida Parkway, **Orlando**, FL 32821, which is near **Sea World** on the northeast corner of Central Florida Parkway and Orangewood ...
About Us · Directions · Prayer · Connect

Fig. 3.2 Google search for churches near SeaWorld Orlando showing

In the screenshot on the previous page, notice how the keyword phrase "Church Near Sea World" is used in the page title at the top of the search result? Using unique keywords in the title of each page on your website helps search engines to determine what the page is all about and if it is relevant to the search query typed in by the person conducting the search. In this case, the page title actually became the text in the link that Google displayed. Beneath that is what Google calls a "snippet". The content for the snippet can be gathered form the web page's meta description tag or from the content of the page itself. In this case, the words "Sea World" are boldened by Google to show the user that this page is relevant to what they are looking for. Below the snippet are links to other pages on the site. These links are displayed to show the user other information that they may find on this website. The links are randomly chosen by Google from pages internally linked from the page that is displayed.

From the example on the previous page, you can see how important it is to include words and phrases in key places on your website that are the same or similar to the words phrases that potential church visitors may be searching for. Grant Hignight was the pastor of Central

Parkway Baptist Church when this screenshot was taken. He optimized his website around words related to SeaWorld because his church is located one block east of SeaWorld Orlando and he wanted to reach out to tourists who are looking for a church to visit while on vacation in Orlando. Now, every week the church is able to minister to people from all over the world who find Central Parkway Baptist by conducting a Google search for "church near Seaworld."

Here are some of the other things that your webservants can do to affect your church's search engine rankings. Encourage other quality websites to link to yours without paying for links. Make sure that your website is easy to navigate, loads quickly and looks good on mobile devices. Make sure that your website uses a responsive design that automatically adjusts to the screen size of any device. Responsive design websites generally look good and are easy to use on phones, tablets, laptops, desktops, and large screen television monitors. Search engines sometimes reward responsive design websites with higher ranking when someone searches from a mobile device. This is important because people now spend more than 60% of their time on the internet on mobile devices[xvi].

What do you do if you have a new website or

if your website is just not ranking well in search engines? First of all, know that search engine companies want to know about your website and its content. If your website is relevant to what people are searching for, if you have a quality site with a high level of trust and your website enhances the end user experience, search engines want to help you promote your church website and to deliver your content to searchers. The major search engines have developed several tools to help you help them to discover your quality content.

Are you intentionally or unintentionally hiding your website and its content from search engines? A common mistake that web developers make can keep your web content from being indexed by search engines. Failure to update the robots.txt files on your website can keep your web pages from being crawled by search engine software. These files give instructions to search engines, telling them which pages should and should not be crawled. You can check to see which of your pages are included in the Google index by conducting a search that looks like this: site:mychurchwebsite.com. Replace the generic URL with your church's actual URL. If you see a message related to robots.txt, you may be blocking your own website. You should contact your web developer to get your robots.txt files updated.

Most search engines allow you to submit a listing of all of your website's pages via an xml sitemap. A sitemap is a web page that lists all of the pages of your website. An xml sitemap is specially formatted for search engines. The major search engines have agreed upon a sitemap protocol that can be found at www.SiteMaps.org. Submitting a sitemap will not guarantee that any of your web pages will be crawled or indexed by the search engines, but it surely helps. Your website should also have a visible html sitemap that is linked from the global footer of your website. An html sitemap allows website visitors to see a listing of all of your web pages. A good practice is to show your html sitemap on your "not found" or 404 page. By doing this, a website visitor that clicks on a link to a page that no longer exists will see a listing of all of your pages instead of a scary error message.

Your church website may contain information about events, locations and other pertinent information that search engines like to display next to or below search results. You can draw attention to this information by using microdata markup. Microdata markup is special code that your web developer can include on your website that helps search engines to determine the kind of information that is contained on your website[xvii]. Some of this information can get special treatment by search engines that helps your website to stand out on search engine results pages. Try doing an internet search for "lasagna recipe." Your search will likely return some results that include a picture of lasagna along with ingredients, cooking times, etc. Other results don't have this information listed. Which ones are you most likely to click? Just like the sitemap protocol, the major search engines have agreed on a structured data markup protocol. Ask your website developer to visit www.Schema.org and see what types of web content can get special attention.

If your church website has a built-in blogging platform, you most likely have access to RSS feeds. RSS stands for Really Simple Syndication. It allows you to broadcast blogs, news feeds and podcasts. By utilizing RSS feeds, you enable internet searchers to subscribe to your website's syndicated content and receive automatic updates anytime you update your web content. Using Google's free FeedBurner.com tool can help you to optimize your website's RSS feeds. Feedburner will allow you to turn an ordinary blog feed into an audio or video podcast. If your church tech team records your pastor's sermons each week, you can easily turn these sermons into podcasts simply by linking to the sermon audio or video file to a blog post and optimizing the blog RSS feed in Feedburner. You can then submit this RSS feed to podcast directories such as iTunes, where users can subscribe to the podcast and have each sermon automatically delivered to their computer, phone, or mp3 player. If your church has its own app, you can use RSS feeds to automatically update the app content directly from the church website. You can also use RSS feeds to "ping" search engines to let them know that your website has new content.

Search engine companies provide these free tools to help you let them know about your important website content. When you use these tools, you help search engines to accomplish their goal to index the world's information and make it available to internet searchers. Search Engine Optimization is good stewardship of your church's time and resources as well as a good missional strategy.

When it comes to Search Engine Optimization, there is no silver bullet that will give your website a boost. Search engines rely on hundreds of ranking signals and they are constantly updating their algorithms to stay ahead of the spammers and to improve the user experience. Websites that have fresh, well written content that meets the needs of their target audiences usually perform better in search results than those that fail in these areas. Quality websites are often shared on social media and are linked to from other quality websites, thus increasing their thrust level and search engine ranking. However, SEO may not be enough. In chapter three, we will explore an option that allows you to pay your way to the top via Search Engine Marketing.

CHAPTER FOUR
SEARCH ENGINE MARKETING

Search engine companies do not charge money for inclusion in their organic search engine results. So how do these companies make money? They charge for advertising in the top spots above organic search results. Participation in paid advertising programs on search engine results pages is called Search Engine Marketing (SEM). Regardless of your best efforts, getting your church website to rank well on search engine results pages is a difficult process that takes a lot of time. Search Engine Marketing is a way to achieve top ranking in the SERP's fairly quickly. The most popular search engine marketing platform is Google Ads (AdWords.Google.com). Advertising on Google's search engine results pages can start out as a simple, inexpensive project that gets quick results. Since you only pay for the ads when they receive clicks, your church can get a lot of exposure at much lower price than traditional advertising.

I have been using Google ADs pay per click advertising for commercial purposes since its inception. In 2003, I contacted a good friend, Hal Haller, and encouraged him to try Google Ads as an outreach tool for a church he was starting in Lakeland, Florida. I offered to manage the account for him, if he would allow me to use the church as an experiment for search engine marketing. Hal's church was in the process of starting two other churches in the area and we tried out AdWords on all three church plants. No other churches in Polk County Florida were using AdWords at that time. This meant that whenever someone searched for a church in or near Lakeland, Florida, the top three search results on Google were the ads for the three churches that Hal was involved in starting. I still remember a story that Hal shared that represents the effectiveness of search engine marketing for churches. We had decided to target people who were searching for a church in Lakeland regardless of where they lived. We established a small daily budget and set the geographic target for the entire United States. Within days, Hal had received an email from a person who lived in Hawaii. Diane explained that she found the church website while searching for churches in Lakeland on Google. She was impressed that Church of the Highlands was listed at the top of the first search results page. She was contacting Hal to let him know that she was going to be visiting Lakeland and would be in his church the next Sunday. Not only did she visit the church, she actually joined the church after moving to Lakeland. She became a very active member and supporter of the church. She was not the only one, but she was one of those reached who made the whole pay-per-click campaign worthwhile.

The pay-per-click (PPC) advertising process starts out with writing three short lines of ad copy, selecting a landing page and choosing some keywords. The ad copy should be attention getting and relevant to the landing page. The keywords need to be relevant to the ad text copy and the website landing page. The advertiser gets to choose the maximum amount he or she is willing to pay per click and the maximum amount to spend each day. Google ranks the ads in order based on such factors as the maximum cost-per-click, ad quality and the use of ad extensions such as address, phone number, sitelinks and callouts.

Now, here is some really good news for your church: Your church may not have to pay for ads on Google. You can get them free through the Google for non-profits program and Google Ad Grants (www.Google.com/grants). If your church is a recognized IRS 501c3 organization, you can apply for the grant and, if accepted, receive an in-kind donation in the form $10,000 per month in pay-per-click advertising credit. That is $10,000 per month every month that your church remains eligible to receive the grant, or $120,000 per year in free online advertising! Although Google Ads has broader distribution channels than just the Google

SERP's, grant recipients can only advertise on Google.com and not their search partners nor the display network.

Building and maintaining a Google Ads Grant account according to the grant requirements can be time consuming. Your church will need someone to set-up and actively manage your advertising account. Google requires that the account manager login at least once a month and make some kind of change to the advertising account every other month. Your account manager can be anyone that you choose. However, this person needs to understand online advertising and how Google Ads works. The account manager will need to make sure that the ads are relevant to the keywords that trigger your ads and that the ads are relevant to the website landing page. He or she will also need to maintain the account with at least a 5% average click-through-rate for your account's ad campaigns and maintain Google's other quality requirements, which are higher for grant recipients.

Search Engine Marketing campaigns allow churches to advertise in most countries around the world. In Central Florida, we have over 75 million people a year visiting our theme parks and beaches. Some of them are looking for a church to visit while they are on vacation and they often use the internet to search for a church near their hotel before they leave home. So, it only makes sense for churches in our area to advertise world-wide. Ads triggered by keywords like "church near Disney World" have helped some of our local churches to connect with tourists visiting the area.

So, if your church ranks well organically for your important keywords, should you consider Search Engine Marketing? SEM can help your church to claim more real-estate at the top of the search engine results pages. Combining SEO and SEM can help your church to increase website traffic and credibility. Search Engine Marketing can be a quick way to get your church listed at the top of the SERP's. The ad campaigns are fairly easy to set up. However, SEM can become fairly complicated. This is due mainly to the advertising options that the search platforms offer. My experience is that most churches will not take advantage of SEM, even when offered the $10,000 a month Google advertising grant, due to the ongoing complexity of managing an SEM account. Effective advertising campaigns require constant attention to keep SEM atrophy from setting in. Google requires monthly account maintenance in order keep receiving their advertising grant.

CHAPTER FIVE
CHURCH APPS

Where do people spend their time? Jesus found fishermen beside the lake mending their nets. He found a tax collector at his tax collector's booth colleting taxes. Jesus knew how to find people and He met them where they were. On summer evenings in late 1940's rural America, you could be sure that you would find people on their front porches drinking lemonade in their rocking chairs listening to their radios. Meeting people on their front porches was the best evangelism strategy that we had at the time. The missional strategy back then was the same as it is now: go where the people are.

In the early twenty-first century, it is harder to find people in just one place. They are mobile and their consumption of media is mobile. According to the research firm, eMarketer, Americans are spending an average of 3 hours and 43 minutes per day on their phones.[xviii] Reaching people where they are in the digital age means reaching people on their phones and other mobile devices. If they are using apps, then your church should at least have an app.

Applications for mobile devices are

becoming more affordable and practical for churches. With the lower cost of development and broad acceptance, churches are discovering that having a custom app is good stewardship. When you compare the annual cost of a quality app with the cost of printing a church bulletin each week, going digital may be more affordable and more effective for your church than previously realized. Companies like Subsplash are now offering mobile apps for churches with no up-front development cost and a small monthly fee.

With your church app on their phones and tablets, your church members are always connected to the church and each other. All of the church announcements for the week, the entire church calendar, locations for small groups, sermon audio and video, and instant notifications are all easily accessible from almost every mobile device. All of this for less than the cost of printing that weekly bulletin. By making your church's information available to more people where ever they are, you are simply serving them better. Why would your church not want to make this digital switch?

Ok, so not everyone has an app enabled mobile device. You can still print those tree-killing bulletins, you just don't need as many after you convince the majority of your congregation to download and use your church's app. With a little bit of creativity, you can have two-thirds of your regular attenders using your church app in no time at all[xix]. You may be surprised to discover, as one church recently observed, that the group to most enthusiastically accept and use a church app is its senior adults. You may be surprised to discover how many of your current church members appreciate app features such as push notifications and calendar integration.

Your church app can contain unique content separate from the church website. The app can also receive automatic updates from the church website via RSS feeds. We discussed RSS briefly in chapter 3 for the purpose of syndicating website content. RSS feeds can also be used to send web content directly to your church app. It is important to your app users that it constantly has fresh and up-to-date content. Another way to keep your app current is to use the iCal feed from your online church calendar to populate a calendar in your church app. With RSS and iCal, updating the information on your church app is as simple as updating the content on your church website. Individuals can also import church events to their personal calendars with a feature that is common in many church apps.

The RSS feed can be used to send sermon audio directly to users' mobile devices. Anyone with the app can listen to the weekly sermons and encourage others to do so as well. In my experience consulting with churches, I have observed that, on average, a sermon receives three times the number of plays online as the number of people who originally heard the message in person. This is due primarily to the original hearers sharing the online sermon with friends and family.

Most app platforms allow you to send push notifications to your app users. A push notification is like a text message that is broadcast to a wide audience. Push notifications activate the users' phone ringer or vibration whenever you send out a message to app users. Unlike a text message, however, push notifications do not allow for two-way communication. Possible uses of push notifications include emergency communication, event reminders, last-minute schedule changes, daily Bible readings, etc.

Your church app can be synchronized with your church's social network channels so that app users can see all of your social media updates in one place. Your church app users can also use the social features of your app to check-in and to post to their social networks. The app can be used to communicate within the church family inwardly and outwardly to the whole world. By encouraging church members and regular attenders to use their mobile devices to update their social media channels in real time with sermon content and information about church events, you are making it easier for them to connect their friends and family with their church family.

CHAPTER SIX
SOCIAL MEDIA

Stephanie sat there staring at her screen, wondering why no one, not one single person had responded to her post. People didn't realize that she was crying out for help, but she checked her social media page one more time just to see if anyone even acknowledged that she had a tough day. While she was sitting there, already in her pajamas, someone was knocking at the door. It sounded like a friendly knock, but no one had texted her or called to say that they were coming over. So, she continued to ignore the knocking while still wondering if anyone really cared about her. On the other side of the door stood three people who wanted to connect with Stephanie. They wanted to get to know her, build a relationship with her and let her know that God loves her, but she was not going to let them into her life through her front door.

The visitors were from the church that Stephanie had attended a couple of times. They had been trained to show up unannounced at a stranger's home and invite them to church. They had prayed that God would allow them to connect with someone who really needed Him and they were given Stephanie's name as an evangelistic prospect. The visitation team figured that she was home. They could see the lights on, her car in the driveway and they could hear some music playing. When no one came to the door, they realized that they were being ignored and they quietly left feeling disappointed that they were not able to share God's love with someone tonight. Stephanie turned her phone over and set it down on the end table while silently praying that God would heal her of her loneliness and fill her emptiness.

This story could have ended differently if the church that Stephanie had visited had learned and adopted a different approach to outreach. In this scenario, we had one person who wanted to be reached and three people willing to reach her, but Stephanie was not going to respond to an unknown knock at her door. She left an open invitation on her social media page when she posted, "Really, really rough day today." All she wanted was for someone to reply with something like, "Sorry to hear that, what happened?" Then she could share her frustrations and at least know that someone else cared.

Imagine what could have happened if the church that Stephanie attended had coached some of their members on how use social media to share Christ's love with people like Stephanie whose hearts are open, but doors are closed. Now, they may have never found her on social media, but they probably had friends like Stephanie. Friends who needed encouragement or just needed to know that someone cares. We all have real friends who would like to spend more time with us and get to know us better. When it comes to building relationships, the best place to start is with people that we already know.

Christians don't have to be trained to share the Gospel, but they do need to be coached. What is the difference? Training teaches you what to say. Coaching encourages you to share what you know. I speak often in churches where I coach those in attendance to turn on their phones, log onto their favorite social network, check-in and share publicly meaningful points from the message while I am preaching. I don't tell them what to post, but I do encourage them to use social media to share what God is doing in their lives.

My father was seventy-seven years old when he got his first computer. He invited my niece to help him set up his new laptop. One of the first things that she did was to set up a Facebook account for her PaPa. Dad was amazed at how the social network allowed him to connect with family and some friends that he had not seen in years. He also used it to search for new people that he had met at church, restaurants and other places. Since he was not physically able to get around much, Facebook was the best place for him to stay connected.

Every day, around 4 a.m., Dad would post a verse from his morning Bible reading to Facebook. He had no idea how many people were reading and depending on his posts for their daily inspiration until he ended up in the hospital for several days. When he felt well enough to check Facebook from his hospital bed, he was surprised at all of the comments from people who were checking to see if he was ok. They all knew that something must be wrong, because Walt was so faithful at posting his daily scripture reading.

Facebook is simply a form of social media that allows people to express themselves in words, pictures and video while interacting with friends, family and perfect strangers. Facebook and other forms of social media help to enhance personal relationships and to create new ones. Facebook alone has over 2.38 billion active monthly users.[xx] That is over ¼ of the world's population!

Regarding social media usage in the United States, Pew Research breaks down social media usage by platform:

- 71% of online adults use Facebook
- 19% of online adults use Twitter

- 17% use Instagram
- 21% use Pinterest
- 22% use LinkedIn[xxi]

The bottom line is that a lot of people are using social media as a tool for interacting with other people. Connecting with people and sharing important information via social media is considered to be a socially acceptable activity in today's American culture. Social media has become the new front porch for conversation in America. LifeWay research was able to find a direct correlation with churches who are more publicly outreach-oriented, develop leaders and have a digital online presence seeing more people come to Christ than those who do not:

> Essentially, we found that churches who are prioritizing a public and digital presence, who have intentional outreach activities and programs, and who are investing in developing lay leaders are all much more likely to be churches who see higher numbers of people make commitments for Christ.[xxii]

To be missional in America is to be on social media. While speaking at a church planting conference in Miami, I was asked if it was really important for mission leaders to be on Facebook. My answer was, "If the people you are trying to reach are on Facebook, then you need to be on Facebook." Social media is no longer an option for missional Christians. Other forms of social media can also interface with Facebook, making it relatively easy to manage several social media accounts from one platform. Dr. Jennifer Bennett suggests these seven ways to be missional on social media:

1. Offer hope and encouragement.
2. Offer to pray for someone.
3. Become known for who you are for, rather than what you are against.
4. Share how God is speaking to you.
5. Be intentional.
6. Turn your words into actions.
7. Remember it is not our job to change people.[xxiii]

At a minimum, pastors and church leaders should have a personal Facebook profile. A personal Facebook account allows a pastor to be transparent and relational. Sharing relevant personal information with church attenders and the general public helps to avoid the pedestal syndrome where pastors are seen as super-Christians and out of touch with regular folks. From their own personal profiles, church leaders can manage their church's Facebook organization page. The church Facebook page is less about the pastor and more about the church family as a whole. The page can have multiple managers who post content, engage with followers, and promote the church to the world.

Facebook is a great place to showcase the community aspect of the church and to let the world know what the church is all about. Images and videos often speak louder than words, so let the world see your church through Facebook.

Facebook is also a great place to promote church events. You can utilize the built-in events feature to showcase and invite people to your events. Facebook is also a cost-effective means of advertising your church to the general public. You can "boost" your Facebook posts in the newsfeed of people that you are targeting. In Chapter 7 we will discuss using live video from social media platforms to live stream Sunday services, special events and personal messages from church leaders.

One of my favorite social media platforms is one that does not get much recognition as a social media platform at all, but it pre-dates Facebook, Twitter, Instagram, Pinterest and many of the more popular ones. When I first discovered Meetup.com, their stated purpose was to get people off of the internet and meeting together face to face. I love attending and hosting Meetup groups, because it is a great way to meet new people, develop friendships, share information and love on people who need Jesus. Meetup.com is a social media platform where people can connect online and meet face to face to talk about topics of common interest or to participate in activities such as hiking, bike-riding, photography and just about anything else that you can think of.

I decided to start a Meetup group after reading the parable of the Good Samaritan in Luke 10: 25-37. Jesus told this parable in response to a question, "And who is my neighbor?" (v. 29b). I had just moved my family from Texas to Florida and we were trying to get to know our neighbors. Other than learning their names, we were not very successful in getting to know anyone in our new neighborhood. I finally realized that we really didn't have much in common with any of the people who lived near us. But, while reading this passage in Luke, it struck me that Jesus did not define neighbor as someone who lives near you. On the contrary, He answered the question with the parable of the Good Samaritan. In this parable, Jesus showed that a neighbor could be anyone you meet with whom you have the opportunity to serve, show mercy, or otherwise demonstrate the love of Christ. I remember praying and asking God to show me some people that I could be neighborly with. God answered my prayer by bringing to mind a group of people with whom I had a common interest and unlimited opportunities to serve them.

The next week, I started a Meetup group for small business entrepreneurs in a local coffee house. I know a few things about entrepreneurs because of my work with church planters. I created a new group on Meetup.com and simply announced the first Meetup to other Meetup users. The website automatically notified people in my area that a new Meetup group was starting nearby. Within a few days, about 30 people had joined my online group and about a dozen RSVP'd for our first face to face Meetup. On the day of our first Meetup, seven people actually showed up. None of us had ever met before that day, but since we all had a common interest, we were willing to spend some time together, getting to know one another and sharing what we know.

At our first Meetup, each person introduced themselves and some handed out their business cards. I started out by saying, "My name is Mark Weible and I am the Director of Church Planting for Greater Orlando Baptist Association." It is not often that a small business owner meets a director of church planting for a Baptist association, so my introduction generated a lot of questions such as, "What does a church planting director do?" I explained what I do by saying something that created an immediate connection with each person in the group. I said, "I coach and train entrepreneurial pastors who start new churches from scratch."

Other questions followed like "How do new churches get started?" Most of the participants were intrigued when I talked about recruiting team members, developing partners, gathering in homes, casting vision, developing launch strategies, etc. These are things that many of them were doing in their start-up businesses. Answering their questions also gave me an opportunity to talk about the nature of a church. Some of the group members thought that churches started with buildings first and then looked for people to fill them. I was able to share with them that churches are made up of people who believe in Christ, worship Him, and share His message of salvation through faith in Him and that these activities do not require a building or even a permanent location.

We met once a month for two hours at a time to discuss search engine optimization and other internet marketing strategies for small businesses. The format was simple, I facilitated a discussion group where members were encouraged to bring a list of their best practices and questions to ask other members. I did not prepare any material to teach or train, I simply started each Meetup by asking the attendees to introduce themselves, tell the group what they did for a living and share what they hoped to get from or to contribute to the group. The introductions led to discussions and soon we became a community of entrepreneurs helping one another. I led this group for eleven years before it began to fizzle out. Over the years, I was able to connect with over 1700 people online. Our monthly Meetups ranged in size from four to forty people at any given time and I had numerous opportunities to share the gospel with people that I had met along the way.

There are several ways that churches can utilize social media to get people together face to face for developing relationships and community. Churches can offer to host offline meetings for existing groups in their facilities or they can create their own community events to promote on social media platforms. Opening up your church building to the community has enormous benefits to the church. First of all, it gets the name of the church out into the community both online and by word of mouth. Second, it shows people in your area that the church is a part of the community at large and can contribute in so many ways toward the betterment of the community. Third, it gets people onto your property and into your buildings so that your physical location becomes more familiar. Now, don't expect people to start attending your church's worship services simply because they attended a community event in your building during the week. But, when people become more familiar with your location, they are more likely to attend when they are invited.

Church members can also create offline social groups that meet in local places of business. Sometimes people are more likely to attend meetings that are not held in church facilities, especially if they come from a non-Christian background. The Meetup group that I started met in coffee houses, restaurants, on a university campus and in our church building. We had been meeting together for several years before I suggested meeting at our church facilities. Since I had built a relationship of trust with the members of the group, most of them had no problem meeting at the church. Some of them did express to me that they felt uncomfortable meeting there, but since the Meetup was creating value for them, they continued to attend and participate

CHAPTER SEVEN
VIDEO

My parents were heavily involved in our church when I was a kid. Mom was a Sunday School teacher and Dad was a deacon. Dad was usually the first person to arrive and unlock the church building on Sunday mornings and one of the last ones to leave. As a family, we participated in everything the church had to offer. We were there for Sunday School, morning worship, discipleship training evening worship and youth activities. Including driving back and forth, we were committed to at least eight hours on Sundays alone. When you add in Tuesday night visitation, teacher's meetings, prayer meetings on Wednesday nights, and then sprinkle in some committee meetings on the other nights of the week and the occasional work days on Saturdays at the church, we were all in at 12 to 20 hours per week. Special events like revival services, Bible study series and Vacation Bible School could easily add another 10 to 20 hours. While I appreciated our church, there were times that I resented not having time to rest on Sundays and not having any time leftover for just being a family.

Most churches today, would not even dare to ask even their most committed church members to keep a schedule like that. Families need to time to be together and they need time to be a part of the community in which they live. And, people today do not have that much free time to give. So, churches have to be careful with what they ask of their members. For our own spiritual development and to foster community within the church body, we still need to worship together, study the Bible together, disciple one another and minister to the community. We still need church members to volunteer their time to carry out the essential functions and administrative needs of the church. In order to do all of this, we need to find ways to work smarter with the technology that we have available to us. Additionally, we are trying to reach people in a culture that has very little available time. Therefore, our outreach strategies have to work smarter as well.

In addition to the digital tools that we've already discussed, many churches have found practical uses for online video. Video is a powerful medium. Second only to face-to-face communication, video is the next best thing to actually being there. Through video people can hear the inflection in your voice, see the emotion on your face, read your body language and watch your presentations and demonstrations. If we are going to go where the people are, then video is where we must go. According to Cisco, by 2022, video will account for 82% of all internet usage.[xxiv] Not only are people consuming more video online, they are watching more of it on their phones and watching less on TV. This represents a tremendous opportunity for churches to connect with people in a way that they want to be reached.

In 2015, Facebook started offering live streaming to their users. In an instant, anyone could take out a cell phone and begin broadcasting live video with fairly decent quality to all of the world. This allowed people to share spontaneous live videos of anything from vacations, public events, wedding proposals, gender reveal parties and so on. Soon, some churches started live streaming their worship services and special events. The early statistics were amazing. Churches were seeing 3-5 times more video views than actual church attendance. Some pastors seized the opportunity to send out more personal messages to their members and prospects. I remember watching Pastor David Uth of First Baptist Church of Orlando doing a live stream from his home prior to the arrival of Hurricane Irma in 2017. That video remains one of the most watched videos that the church has produced and it was done "on the fly" with his cell phone. The purpose of the video was to announce that the church was not having public worship services that Sunday due to the arrival of the hurricane. However, Pastor Uth also used that opportunity to help encourage people by letting them know that not only was he praying for them, but other pastors around the country were leading their people to pray for them during this time of pending natural disaster.

There are several reasons why video is growing so rapidly online. First is availability. Almost anyone can produce a live or recorded video using a device that they carry with them every day. The second is cost, as there is no added cost to producing, hosting and sharing video other than what they've already paid for their phone and data service. Third, there is quality. Most phones on the market today have the capability of producing higher quality video than most TV reporters had available to them twenty years ago. Fourth, expectations are low for personally produced video on mobile devices. No one is expecting your spontaneous video to have a high production value. Perhaps most important is the fact that people are watching all kinds of streaming video on their phones, computers and televisions. If we want to go where the people are, then we must go video.

There are several free and inexpensive places to host or stream your online video. We've already talked briefly about live streaming from Facebook, but there are many other ways to do online video. The platform that you choose should be related to your purpose. While Facebook may be the best platform for live streaming, you probably want to consider YouTube or Vimeo for pre-recorded video. The most popular video platform by far is YouTube. YouTube has over 1 billion users and over 400 hours of video are being uploaded to YouTube every month.[xxv]

YouTube is actually owned by Google and is a video search engine in and of itself. In fact, YouTube is the second largest search engine and search results from YouTube often show up at the top of Google's search engine results pages. So, if you want your video to be found online, then you will want your video to be on YouTube. You can both live stream from YouTube and upload pre-recorded video. Video posted on YouTube is easy to share on other social media platforms and can be embedded on your church website and other sites as well. You can use YouTube for a variety of purposes, such as broadcasting your weekly services, doing video devotionals, hosting online meetings or sending more personalized video messages.

Church meetings don't always have to happen in person. In the digital age, many of your church members are used to having online meetings at work. And would probably prefer that the church adapt this technology as well. If you are going to be hosting an online meeting or video conference, you may want to consider a platform such as Zoom, GoToMeeting or something similar. Video conferencing platforms allow for live online meetings that can also be recorded and played back for those who missed the meeting. They allow single or multiple presenters with the option for attendees to chime in from their own devices. They allow for screen-sharing so that using PowerPoint or other presentation software is fairly simple. Popular video conferencing software usually includes file sharing, making it easy to send attachments to meeting participants.

Another use for online video that continues to gain in popularity is online courses. More and more education in public schools and universities is happening online and many businesses are now doing their employees training online. So, it only makes sense for churches to adopt this technology for Bible study, discipleship classes, leadership training development and ministry training. There are many possible uses for online training and there are several training platforms available for churches.

The one that I use most often is called Kajabi. I

like Kajabi because it is all-inclusive. On this platform, you can create video and text-based online classes, add quizzes to test the students' knowledge and retention, as well as create closed online communities. Kajabi also includes an email marketing platform as well as a website platform. There is a cost for using Kajabi, but they offer a free trial period. It is worth a look at www.FreeKajabi.com.

Whether your church chooses to use video to do outreach, discipleship, provide encouraging ministry or to train and develop current and future leaders, you are providing a service to your church and community that they will appreciate and support. There is one commodity that we all seem to have less of today and that is time. While face to face interaction is always best, video can become second-best and when time is of the essence, video may be your only choice for connecting people and growing your church.

CHAPTER EIGHT
PUTTING IT ALL TOGETHER

How in the world can anyone keep up with posting to a church website, multiple social media accounts, and video platforms, all the while interacting with the people who post comments and have questions? No one can. It takes a team of people to do all of that. If you are a pastor reading this, I don't want you to feel overwhelmed. I don't want you to add anything new to your plate. Your only task is to find someone to lead your digital outreach team and to recruit some passionate members who will carry on this ministry.

Who should serve on your digital outreach team? Obviously, you need people-oriented people who can read, write and communicate well. You need people who are positive, compassionate, and graceful. Your digital outreach team will be the face of the church. They will be the first point of contact for almost anyone who visits your church's worship service for the first-time. Think of them as digital greeters. It is not necessary for them to be technology people or even social media experts. However, each of your team members should have a history of using social media and other online tools in a positive, responsible way.

The purpose of your digital outreach team is to start and grow relationships and develop a sense of community with people online and often before there has been any face to face interaction with people from the church. Your digital outreach team should develop digital pathways for connecting with the various groups of people that your church encounters online. Pathways are simply a series of steps that you would like for people to take in the process of becoming a disciple of Jesus Christ in the context of your local church ministry. One of the pathways could look something like this:

> Internet search > landing page > contact form > email notification > team member response > additional questions > appropriate connection > follow-up > invitation > face to face event > evaluation > thank you > resource recommendation > follow-up > gospel conversation > small group > worship gathering > ministry involvement > leader training > multiplication

When developing pathways, team members should put themselves in the situation of the person with whom a relationship is being built. Ask, questions like, "If I were this person, what actions would I find encouraging and what would I perceive to be annoying." In other words, try to determine the best way to show love to the 99% of the people who visit your church website or social media page, but never attend your church. The team should make it a personal challenge to help each person to feel like they are valued, that they are wanted and that there is a community of people who loves them and wants them to be a part of something wonderful. In order to be effective, the digital outreach team must work hard at building trust through love and not letting anyone feel like they have fallen through the cracks. Remember the reversed engineered evangelism process that we discussed in chapter one? An evangelism pathway could look like this:

> Prayer > Encounter > Relationship > Serve > Love > Share >Disciple > Lead > Multiply

Pathways are not meant to be totally linear. Anyone can enter a pathway at any point and could circle back around to pick up any steps that were missed. We must always remember that we are dealing with people. God made each one of them different from the next and He loves them more than we do. Our objective is not to run people through a process. We are here to be companions on a spiritual journey. Pathways are merely visualizations that help us to help people who need us to lead them into a relationship with the God who created them.

Community begins with relationships and relationships start with conversations. So, in order to foster community, we must encourage conversations. Online conversations can happen most easily on social media platforms where people like, share and comment on content. Conversations can also happen on church websites. An effective church website is one that encourages conversations that lead to relationships. When web content is written in a way that encourages interaction, conversations are more likely. If your team views the church website merely as a place to post information, then conversation is stifled. Bear in mind that a person's first interaction with your church may be due to an internet search which lands them on a random page of your church website and not necessarily the home page. The challenge for your team is to create content that fosters conversation and to be creative in how that conversation can take place. Website visitors can be encouraged to email a contact person for more information, complete an online form, sign up for a newsletter subscription, download a document, join a social media group, comment on a blog post or even call the church office. Remember that communication is a two-way process, so be sure to allow for and encourage online conversations in any way that you can.

Conversations that lead to relationships that

create and enhance community is what we want to accomplish with the digital tools that we have at our resource. When conversations occur, it is the responsibility of the digital outreach team to encourage the development of an on-going relationship that leads to further conversations that build trust and demonstrate Christ's love. Community can begin to take shape online, but we must not limit it there. In order for real community to take place, we must get people together face to face. Now it is possible that your team will create community with people who are not geographically near any of your church gatherings, perhaps they live in another country, or on another continent. In those situations, we want to connect them with a church in their area. For several years, I served as an online missionary with Global Media Outreach. My task was to respond to people who had interacted with an online gospel presentation and guide them through their next steps. One of those steps was to connect them with a local church. I would ask them if they knew of any Bible-teaching churches in their area. If they didn't know of any, I would ask them for permission to contact our denominational missionary in that region and pass along their information. Your digital outreach team can do the same thing with people who live out of town.

For people in your area, you are going to

want to connect them with a discipleship group where face to face relationships can happen and spiritual nurturing can take place. Ideally, you would have a representative of each of your small groups serving on your digital outreach team so that they can personally invite a web contact to a discipleship group. When an invitation is given to attend a worship gathering at your church, make sure that the person knows that someone from the team will be there to greet them on their first Sunday, show them around the campus, get their kids checked in, help with refreshments, etc.

Having a digital outreach team that monitors all of the church's internet assets, creates engaging content, fosters online conversations, and helps to create a sense of community can result in the church reaching and discipling more people using the tools that God has already given us. When the church engages the unreached community in this way, not only is the church offering hope for hurting people in a way that they want to be reached, but it is also creating opportunities for people to serve using their giftedness and abilities in new ways.

APPENDIX
RESOURCES FOR BEING THE
CHURCH
IN THE DIGITAL AGE

www.OurChurch.Website – An easy to use content management system website platform that offers unlimited pages, storage, bandwidth, users, and an online store with unlimited digital and physical products for a fixed price of $29 per month. OurChurch.website is owned and managed by the Renovate Group, which publishes this book.

www.Google.com/grants - Offers $10,000 per month in in-kind online advertising credits to churches and non-profit organizations.

www.Google.com/business - A free service for listing your church in the Google local directory that often results in top of the page search results (the Google 3 pack). Similar services are offered by Bing at www.BingPlaces.com and Yahoo at www.SmallBusiness.Yahoo.com/local.

www.Google.com/webmasters - A suite of free resources available to churches that help to maximize your website visibility on Google's search engine result pages. Similar services are available from Bing and Yahoo at www.Bing.com/toolbox/webmaster.

www.Analytics.Google.com – A free service from Google that measures website traffic with important metrics such as traffic source, visitor count, page views, time on site, bounce rate, conversion rate and more.

www.Google.com/nonprofits - A suite of tools available to churches and other non-profit organizations. Included is the Google Ads Grant, which is an in-kind advertising grant from Google for up to $10,000 per month in advertising credits on Google's search results pages.

www.ads.google.com/home/tools/keyword-planner/ - A tool that helps you to research keywords to use on your website. This tool requires a Google Ads account.

www.FeedBurner.com – A free tool from Google for optimization and promotion of RSS feeds. This resource can be used to help syndicate blogs and podcasts to various readers and directories. It also includes an email subscription tool.

www.FreeKajabi.com – A fourteen-day free trial of the Kajabi platform which includes web hosting, tools for creating and hosting online video courses and email marketing.

www.CVI.Report – A core values
psychometric assessment that helps
individuals and teams to identify their core
values and to work toward greater harmony.

www.Renovate.Digital – an online resource for
church revitalization training offered by the
Renovate Group.

www.BlessEveryHome.com -   A free resource that
helps you to pray for your neighbors by name.

ABOUT THE AUTHOR

Mark Weible serves as the Director of Church Planting for the Greater Orlando Baptist Association. He is also the co-founder and Strategic Director of the Renovate National Church Revitalization Conference and Directional Leader for Reproducing Churches.

Mark is an experienced Search Engine Optimizer and Google Ads Professional. He is a certified Leadership Development Facilitator and Biblical DISC practitioner through Lead Like Jesus. Mark is also a trained Core Values Index Super User and a co-developer of the Church Planter and Church Revitalizer Top Performer Profiles in partnership with Exos Advisors. He is assistant editor, web traffic manager and a regular contributing writer to the Church Revitalizer Magazine. Mark is a trainer and conference speaker on the subjects of church planting, church revitalization, leadership development, search engine optimization and online marketing.

Mark and his family live in Orlando, Florida where he serves as an elder in his church.

NOTES

[i] Matthew 9: 37b

[ii] II Corinthians 4:7

[iii] Tom Cheyney, Steve Sells, *Life After Death: A Strategy to Bring New Life to a Dead Church!* Orlando, FL: Renovate Publishing Group, 2019, page 122.

[iv] Chuck Kelly at Greater Orlando Baptist Association Annual Celebration, October 14, 2013 at First Baptist Church of Kissimmee.

[v] Alex L. Goldfayn, *Evangelist Marketing: What Apple, Amazon, and Netflix Understand About Their Customers (That Your Company Probably Doesn't)*, (Dallas: BenBella Books, 2011), xiv.

[vi] Acts 17:29

[vii] John 17:34

[viii] Acts 17:15

[ix] John 21:5

[x] Thom S. Rainer, "10 Things Churches Can Do Better"

https://www.lifeway.com/en/articles/10-things-churches-can-do-better

xi Neil Patel, "The Number One Reason 99% of Your Visitors Don't Buy from You [Fast Conversion Rate Optimization]", https://www.youtube.com/watch?v=3yT22HOenzE

xii Danny Sullivan, "Internet Top Information Resource, Study Finds," Search Engine Watch, February 5, 2001, searchenginewatch.com/article/2067636/Internet-Top-Information-Resource-Study-Finds

xiii www.Google.com/Webmasters/Tools

xiv Matthew 28:18

xv Acts 1:8

xvi Andrew Lipsman, Comscore, "Major Mobile Milestones in May: Apps Now Drive Half of All Time on Digital," June 25, 2014, comscore.com/Insights/Blog/Major-Mobile-Milestones-in-May-Apps-Now-Drive-Half-of-All-Time-Spent-on-Digital.

xvii Google, "About rich snippets and structured data,"https://support.google.com/webmasters/answer/99170?hl=en.

xviii Wendy Lee, "People spend more time on mobile devices than TV, firm says", Los Angeles Times, June 5, 2019. https://www.latimes.com/business/la-fi-ct-people-spend-more-time-on-mobile-than-tv-20190605-story.html

xix Nielsen, "What's Empowering The New Digital Consumer?", February 10, 2014, www.nielsen.com/content/corporate/us/en/insight..s/news/2014/whats-empowering-the-new-digital-consumer.html

xxStatista. https://www.statista.com/statistics/264810/number-of-monthly-active-facebook-users-worldwide/

xxi Pew Research, "Social Networking Fact Sheet,"www.pewinternet.org/fact-sheets/social-networking-fact-sheet.

xxii Ed Stetzer, Micah Fries, and Daniel Im. "The State of Church Planting in the U.S.", LifeWay Research and NewChurches.com, 2015 pg 13.

xxiii Jennifer M. Bennett, #BEWORTHFOLLOWING: How to Be Different and Influence People in a Crowded Social World, United States: DrJenBennett, 2017.

[xxiv] Cisco Visual Networking Index: Forecast and Trends, 2017–2022 White Paper, https://www.cisco.com/c/en/us/solutions/collateral/service-provider/visual-networking-index-vni/white-paper-c11-741490.html.

[xxv] Eagle, W. (n.d.). YouTube Marketing for Dummies. p.8.